Y0-CPE-810

ELBRUS

Rochelle Groskreutz

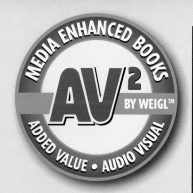

AV² provides enriched content that supplements and complements this book. Weigl's AV² books strive to create inspired learning and engage young minds in a total learning experience.

Your AV² Media Enhanced books come alive with...

Audio
Listen to sections of the book read aloud.

Key Words
Study vocabulary, and complete a matching word activity.

Video
Watch informative video clips.

Quizzes
Test your knowledge.

Embedded Weblinks
Gain additional information for research.

Slideshow
View images and captions, and prepare a presentation.

Try This!
Complete activities and hands-on experiments.

... and much, much more!

Go to **www.av2books.com**, and enter this book's unique code.

BOOK CODE

A V Q 2 6 5 4 2

AV² by Weigl brings you media enhanced books that support active learning.

Published by AV² by Weigl
350 5th Avenue, 59th Floor
New York, NY 10118
Website: www.av2books.com

Library of Congress Cataloging-in-Publication Data
Names: Groskreutz, Rochelle, author.
Title: Elbrus / Rochelle Groskreutz.
Description: New York : AV2 by Weigl, [2019] | Series: Seven summits | Includes index. | Audience: Grade 4 to 6.
Identifiers: LCCN 2019009587 (print) | LCCN 2019017856 (ebook) | ISBN 9781791114091 (multi User ebook) | ISBN 9781791114305 (single User ebook) | ISBN 9781791114077 (hc.: alk. paper) | ISBN 9781791114084 (pbk. : alk. paper)
Subjects: LCSH: Elbrus, Mount (Russia)--Juvenile literature. | Natural history--Russia (Federation)--Elbrus, Mount--Juvenile literature. | Mountain ecology--Russia (Federation)--Elbrus, Mount--Juvenile literature.
Classification: LCC GB542.R9 (ebook) | LCC GB542.R9 G76 2019 (print) | DDC 947.5/2--dc23
LC record available at https://lccn.loc.gov/2019009587

Printed in Guangzhou, China
1 2 3 4 5 6 7 8 9 0 23 22 21 20 19

052019
102318

Editor: Katie Gillespie
Designers: Tammy West and Ana Maria Vidal

Every reasonable effort has been made to trace ownership and to obtain permission to reprint copyright material. The publishers would be pleased to have any errors or omissions brought to their attention so that they may be corrected in subsequent printings.

Photo Credits
Weigl acknowledges Getty Images, Alamy, iStock, Dreamstime, Shutterstock, and Wikipedia Commons as its primary photo suppliers for this title.

ELBRUS

SEVEN SUMMITS

CONTENTS

The Highest View in All of Europe

Between the Black Sea and the Caspian Sea are the Caucasus Mountains. The range extends a total distance of 750 miles (1,200 kilometers). It contains a volcano called Mount Elbrus. Not only is Mount Elbrus the highest of the Caucasus Mountains, it is also the highest peak in all of Europe.

Mount Elbrus has twin cones. Its eastern summit has an **elevation** of 18,356 feet (5,595 meters). The western summit is the higher of the two, at 18,510 feet (5,642 m). Mount Elbrus also has a **saddle** between its two summits, with an elevation of 17,769 feet (5,416 m). People come from all over the world to see this impressive mountain.

Although there are huts on Elbrus, some visitors choose to camp on the mountain instead.

A new cable car opened on Mount Elbrus in April 2009.

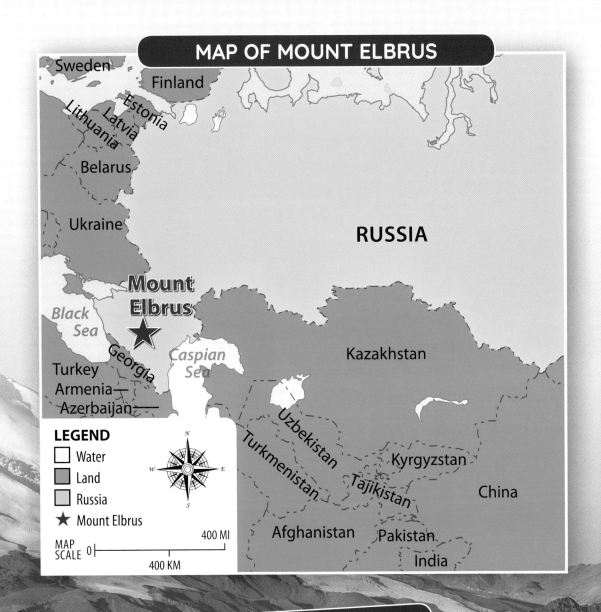

MAP OF MOUNT ELBRUS

Sweden

Finland

Estonia

Latvia

Lithuania

Belarus

Ukraine

RUSSIA

Mount Elbrus ★

Black Sea

Georgia

Caspian Sea

Kazakhstan

Turkey

Armenia—

Azerbaijan—

Uzbekistan

Turkmenistan

Kyrgyzstan

Tajikistan

China

LEGEND

☐ Water
☐ Land
☐ Russia
★ Mount Elbrus

N W E S

Afghanistan

Pakistan

India

MAP SCALE 0 —————— 400 MI
                 400 KM

ELBRUS FACTS

- The Caucasus Mountains are more than 25 million years old.

- Although Mount Elbrus is a volcano, its two giant cones are filled with ice and snow, rather than **lava**.

- Mount Elbrus is covered by 22 **glaciers** that span 53 square miles (138 square km).

- More than 300,000 people safely visit Mount Elbrus each year, yet it is considered one of the world's deadliest mountains.

Where in the World?

Extending across both Europe and Asia, Russia is the largest country in the world, by a significant margin. Russia is so large that it is almost double the size of Canada, the next-largest country. Mount Elbrus is located in southwestern Russia. It is near the border of Georgia, which lies to the south.

The Caucasus Mountains are made up of two ranges called the Lesser Caucasus and the Greater Caucasus. Mount Elbrus is part of the Greater Caucasus range. Visitors to the popular tourist area of Mount Elbrus come through the city of Nalchik, 75 miles (120 km) east, or the town of Mineralnye Vody, 124 miles (200 km) north.

Nalchik is the capital of the Russian republic of Kabardino-Balkariya.

Climbers often attach spiky crampons to their boots to help keep from slipping along frozen trails.

Puzzler

Mount Elbrus is the highest mountain on the continent of Europe. The highest mountains for all of the continents, sometimes called the "seven summits," are listed below. Using an atlas or the internet, match the mountain to the correct continent.

CONTINENTS
1. North America
2. South America
3. Europe
4. Antarctica
5. Asia
6. Australasia
7. Africa

MOUNTAINS
A. Mount Everest
B. Denali
C. Mount Aconcagua
D. Mount Elbrus
E. Carstensz Pyramid
F. Mount Kilimanjaro
G. Vinson Massif

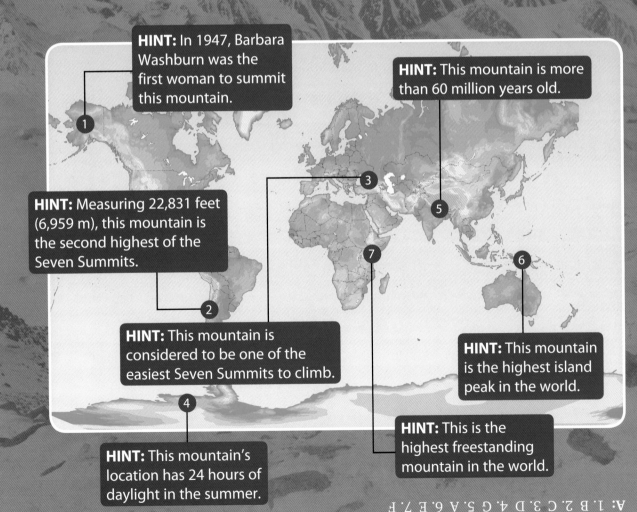

HINT: In 1947, Barbara Washburn was the first woman to summit this mountain.

HINT: This mountain is more than 60 million years old.

HINT: Measuring 22,831 feet (6,959 m), this mountain is the second highest of the Seven Summits.

HINT: This mountain is considered to be one of the easiest Seven Summits to climb.

HINT: This mountain is the highest island peak in the world.

HINT: This mountain's location has 24 hours of daylight in the summer.

HINT: This is the highest freestanding mountain in the world.

A: 1. B 2. C 3. D 4. G 5. A 6. E 7. F

Forged in Lava and Ice

Nearly 250,000 years ago, a giant, fiery lava explosion happened. It created a caldera, or volcanic crater, between 9 and 11 miles (14 and 17 km) in diameter. Mount Elbrus formed inside this caldera.

The unique shape of Mount Elbrus happened over time. Its twin slopes were once two active volcano cones spewing molten lava. Now, these two slopes are packed with snow and ice.

Glaciers covering Mount Elbrus help feed flowing rivers and lakes in the area. Dams help prevent melting glaciers from causing flooding. In 2006, a glacier dam broke in one of the lakes and caused a flood down the mountain. No one was hurt, but the flood destroyed a nearby resort.

Greater Azau Glacier is found on Elbrus's south slopes.

Active or Extinct?

Mount Elbrus is the largest volcano in Europe. Many experts once agreed that it is extinct, since the volcano has not erupted since 50 AD. That changed when scientists discovered an active magma chamber on its eastern slope in 1984. This chamber is a large pool of liquid rock, or magma, under Earth's **crust**.

The magma underneath Mount Elbrus will likely never reach the surface. However, this chamber discovery means that the volcano is considered **dormant**, rather than extinct. Visitors may see steam and smell sulfur gas on its eastern slope. This happens because magma contains gases that can seep up through the surface of any volcano.

Magma that reaches Earth's surface through a volcano's vent, or opening, becomes lava.

Plentiful Plant Life

Plant life is rich and diverse in the Mount Elbrus region. This area is home to 6,400 different **species** of plants. Most grow at the base of the slopes, along the rivers, and in the valleys near the mountain.

Lichens grow close to the edges of glaciers on Mount Elbrus. They cover stones and can be found in many colors, such as green, gray, brown, and yellow. The valleys and bottom slope areas of the mountain are covered in a thick forest of trees. Growing in this rich soil are dozens of varieties, including pine, birch, aspen, cherry, maple, linden, willow, and ash.

Many bushes grow in the forests below Mount Elbrus, such as juniper, barberry, and currant. The surrounding meadows are home to flowers in a variety of colors, including pink, blue, red, and yellow. From dainty white snowdrop blossoms to rhododendrons as big as a person's hand, flowers blanket the landscape.

Snowdrops typically blossom in late winter or early spring.

Dragonwort and Rose Trees

Dragonwort and rose trees are among the most distinctive types of flowering plants that grow in the Mount Elbrus region. The scientific name for dragonwort is *polygonum bistorta*. This hearty plant is found in meadows and near streams below Mount Elbrus. Russians often call it "serpentine" because of the snake-like shape of its roots. The starchy dragonwort root has long been used for food in Europe. Dragonwort roots can also be used for medicinal purposes, to stop bleeding, as an antibacterial, and to treat digestive issues.

Rose trees are actually rhododendrons. The name rhododendron comes from the Greek words *rodon*, which means "rose," and *dendron*, which means "tree." All the parts of rhododendrons are dangerous, so unlike dragonwort, they should not be ingested.

A dragonwort's flowering stem can reach a height of about 30 inches (75 centimeters).

Animal Life on Mount Elbrus

More than 700 species of **vertebrate** animals live in the Mount Elbrus region. Goat antelopes graze below the peaks of these snow-capped mountains. These include the chamois and the West Caucasian tur.

The surrounding forests are home to many animals, such as wild boar, deer, brown bears, foxes, weasels, and lynxes. Living along the forest floor are several other animals, including hares, wild turkeys, ground squirrels, polecats, and pine martens.

The rivers and lakes below Mount Elbrus are full of brown trout, northern pike, and many other types of freshwater fish and aquatic species. Flying overhead are rare birds, including the peregrine falcon, Caucasian black grouse, parrot crossbill, tawny owl, and white-throated dipper. It is even possible to spot endangered predators near Mount Elbrus, such as the golden eagle and bearded vulture.

The alpine chough is a crowlike bird that lives in high mountains. It is recognizable due to its yellow, down-curved bill.

West Caucasian tur

West Caucasian turs are unique to the Mount Elbrus region. They look like a cross between a goat and an antelope. Their bodies are large, but narrow, with short legs. They also have curved horns with deep ridges. West Caucasian turs have a chestnut brown coat, lighter underbellies, and darker legs.

These animals are **nocturnal**. They live in the rugged mountain, cliff, and meadow areas just below the snow line of Mount Elbrus, between 2,640 and 13,200 feet (805 and 4,023 m). For most of the year, males and females live separately in single-sex herds.

West Caucasian turs are **herbivores**. Their diet contains more than 100 different species of plants. They feed on grass and herbs in the summer, and they eat leaves in the winter.

Young West Caucasian turs are taken care of solely by females.

Elbrus's First Explorers

Killar Khashirov was the first person to reach the lower eastern summit of Mount Elbrus, in July 1829. He was a hunter, hired to guide a Russian army scientific expedition. Khashirov was the only one in the group who successfully summited.

The western summit was first reached in July 1874, by a group of five people. They were led by British mountaineer Florence Crauford Grove. The others included local guide Akhia Sottaiev, Englishmen Frederick Gardner and Horace Walker, and Swiss climber Peter Knubel.

Grove, one of the best British climbers at the time, wrote a detailed book about his expedition. It was entitled *The Frosty Caucasus*. The book includes a folding map and photographs taken by Horace Walker.

The Frosty Caucasus was first published in 1875.

Biography
Jordan Romero (1996–)

Jordan Romero was born on July 12, 1996. In third grade, he could not stop thinking about the Seven Summits mural he saw at school. "When I get interested in something, I become a fanatic and learn everything I can about it," said the California native in his book, *No Summit Out of Sight*.

Romero started his Seven Summits journey at the age of 10, when he climbed Mount Kilimanjaro in Africa. He continued to pursue his dream, and by age 15, had set a world record as the youngest person ever to climb all of the Seven Summits. Mount Elbrus was the third summit Romero reached, on July 11, 2007, the day before his 11th birthday.

Romero climbed Mount Everest, the world's highest mountain, in May 2010.

Volcanoes to Visit

People visit volcanoes all around the world. Many of these volcanoes are inactive today. Some volcanoes have not erupted for hundreds or even thousands of years.

Thrihnukagigur
Iceland
Last eruption: more than 4,000 years ago

North America

Atlantic Ocean

Pacific Ocean

South America

Mauna Kea
Hawai'i
Last eruption: 2460 BC

Volcán Mombacho
Nicaragua
Last eruption: 1570 AD

LEGEND
- Water
- Land
- Antarctica
- Volcano

N
W E
S

MAP SCALE 0 ⊢——————⊣ 2,000 MI
2,000 KM

Mount Elbrus
Russia
Last eruption: 50 AD

Guishan Island
Taiwan
Last eruption: 1785 AD

Europe

Asia

Africa

Pacific
Ocean

Indian
Ocean

Australia

Southern
Ocean

Mount Eden
New Zealand
Last eruption:
28,000 years ago

Antarctica

People of Mount Elbrus

The Balkar people live in the Mount Elbrus region. Centuries ago, their ancestors were sheepherders. Many Balkars still make a living today by herding their flocks of sheep.

Originally, the Balkars lived in homes made of mud and wood. Today, their houses are built with brick or stone, with tile or slate roofs. The main language of the Balkar people is a Turkic one called Karachay-Balkar. The most-practiced religion is Islam.

During World War II, which took place from 1939 to 1945, Soviet Union **dictator** Joseph Stalin forced 38,000 Balkar people to leave the region. He accused them of collaborating with **Nazi** Germany. In 1957, they were allowed to return, but it has been difficult for the Balkars to make a good living since then. Many have moved to Nalchik or to Moscow for better education and job opportunities.

Today, there are approximately 100 small villages in the Mount Elbrus area inhabited only by Balkars.

A Knitting Tradition

The traditional Balkar way of life remains today. Most Balkar people are able to make cheese, feed sheep, and work at haymaking. One of the most important skills that Balkars learn is knitting.

Balkar children are taught how to knit as young as six years old. Every day before leaving school, many of them are busy knitting woolen scarves, sweaters, and socks. Balkar families sell their woolen garments and souvenirs at tourist markets in the Mount Elbrus area.

In Balkar culture, it is customary for all members of the family to knit.

Mount Elbrus Timeline

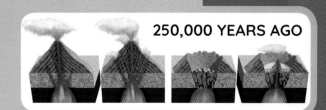

25 MILLION YEARS AGO

Prehistoric

25 million years ago The Caucasus Mountains surrounding Mount Elbrus form.

250,000 years ago Mount Elbrus forms inside a caldera.

250,000 YEARS AGO

170,000 years ago Mount Elbrus forms a second dome and erupts repeatedly, creating a lava buildup that is 1.2 miles (2 km) thick.

60,000 years ago Volcanic eruptions continue, but the current twin slopes of Mount Elbrus are in place.

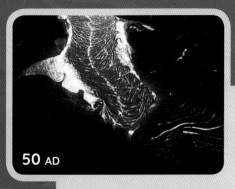

50 AD

Exploration

50 AD Mount Elbrus has its last volcanic eruption.

1829 Khashirov is the first to reach the eastern summit.

1874 Grove's expedition reaches the western summit.

1874

Development

1932 Mount Elbrus's first hut, Priut 11, is built at 13,650 feet (4,160 m).

1959–1976 A cable car system is built to take visitors to 12,500 feet (3,800 m).

1986 Elbrus becomes part of Prielbrusye National Park, one of Russia's protected areas.

1959–1976

1998 Climbers start a fire while cooking that burns down Priut 11.

1932

Present

2007 American Jordan Romero is the youngest person to reach the western summit.

2007

2015 At age 13, Jaahnavi Sriperambuduru of India is the youngest female climber to reach the western summit.

2015

2016 Russians Artyom Kuimov and Sergey Baranov summit Elbrus on all-terrain vehicles (ATVs).

2017 Starting with Mount Elbrus, Swedish photographer Emma Svensson scales the highest mountain in every European country in one year.

Key Issue: Threats to Mount Elbrus

As one of the Seven Summits, Mount Elbrus is a popular mountain climbing and outdoor adventure destination. It is covered with snow year-round, making it an ideal place for climbers, snowboarders, and skiers. However, since the area attracts more visitors each year, there are serious environmental concerns.

The main climbing route is crowded and dirty. Many mountain **crevasses** are filled with plastic bags, water bottles, and wrappers. Some campers leave their trash to pile up rather than taking it with them.

Climate change also threatens the area. Glaciers have been melting steadily there, which causes avalanches, flooding, and mudslides. Avalanches have killed more than 50 visitors to Elbrus since 2002. After a mudslide in 2017, the entire Mount Elbrus area had to be evacuated, and 7,700 people were stranded.

As a result of the 2017 mudslide, part of the asphalt road was destroyed and in need of repair.

Though residents in the Elbrus area welcome tourism, attracting more people there means more pollution. The Prielbrusye National Park surrounding Mount Elbrus was established to protect and conserve the **ecosystem** of the region. The park is located on the peaks and north slope of the central Caucasus Mountains. Mount Elbrus is on the western boundary of the park.

Elbrus was incorporated into Prielbrusye National Park in 1986.

SHOULD MORE TOURIST ATTRACTIONS BE BUILT IN THE MOUNT ELBRUS REGION?

YES	NO
This would give visitors more things to do and more places to stay when visiting the area.	Too many trees will have to be cut down to make room for new hotels and other buildings.
The area would feel less crowded if there were more attractions to accommodate visitors.	Cutting down more trees increases the risk of dangerous avalanches.
More tourism development means more jobs and money for people living in the region.	There is already too much pollution and litter in the area, and more people visiting it will only make things worse.

A Winter Wonderland

People enjoy thrilling winter activities on Mount Elbrus all year long. Prielbrusye National Park is where visitors go for winter sports, as well as for camping, ATV tours, and eco-tours. The area surrounding Mount Elbrus has several valleys and smaller peaks that are also worth exploring.

Mountaineers, skiers, snowboarders, and other tourists flock to the region. Hikers travel trails such as those along Donguz-Orunkel Lake. Some visitors opt to take a cable car ride up and back down Mount Elbrus, simply to enjoy the view.

Although Mount Elbrus offers many outdoor activities, the weather can be harsh and unpredictable at times. Sunny skies can turn to blinding, snowy winds within minutes. Temperatures regularly drop to well below freezing, especially at night. Those who want a break from the cold can visit other attractions, such as the Vladimir Vysotsky Alpine Museum.

Temperatures on Elbrus average 18° Fahrenheit (-8° Celsius) at night during the summer months.

Run to the Sky

Most people climb up mountains slowly, in order to let their bodies adjust to the lower oxygen levels in the air at higher **altitudes**. However, some enjoy the adventure of skyrunning. This extreme sport involves mountain running at an elevation of 6,562 feet (2,000 m) or higher. Skyrunners spend months or even years training in higher altitudes to get their lungs and hearts in shape for such a rigorous event.

Another extreme way to summit peaks such as Mount Elbrus is ski mountaineering. This sport involves climbing mountains either on skis or carrying them, depending on how steep the ascent is, and then descending on skis. Extreme athletes come together at the annual Red Fox Elbrus Race Festival. This international event includes skyrunning, climbing, ski mountaineering, and snowshoeing.

The Red Fox Elbrus Race Festival is held in May.

A Mountain with Many Names

Over time, there have been several stories about Mount Elbrus. These tales have led to many different names for the towering twin slopes. The oldest known name for Mount Elbrus is *Alborz*, a Persian word meaning "High Sentinel or Guard." It comes from an ancient myth.

The Balkar people refer to Mount Elbrus as *Mingi-Tau*, which means "A Thousand Mountains" in their language. The local Turkic people of the Caucasus Mountain range call it *Yalbuz*, meaning "Ice Mane." Another group of local people, who live in the Northwest Caucasian area, call the mountain *Oshkhamakhua*. This means "Mountain of Happiness."

Elbrus's two peaks inspired one of its names, *Sobilus*, a Latin word meaning "pine cone."

Punishment for Prometheus

The Caucasus Mountains are known as the setting for a Greek myth about Zeus and Prometheus. Zeus was the most powerful god, who had many powers. He was recognized for his ability to throw lightning bolts that could cause fires. Prometheus was a **Titan**, who created humankind out of clay and water.

When Zeus mistreated mankind, Prometheus stole fire from him, and gave humankind its power for arts and sciences. This made Zeus angry. To punish Prometheus, Zeus chained him to a mountain. Zeus then sent a long-winged eagle over the mountain to attack Prometheus.

Zeus's son, Heracles, learned what his father had done. Heracles liked Prometheus, and thought that Zeus had gone too far, so he hurried to the mountain. Just in time, Heracles freed Prometheus, then killed the fierce eagle.

The story of Prometheus has been portrayed in art forms ranging from paintings to sculptures.

What Have You Learned?

True or False?

Decide whether the following statements are true or false. If the statement is false, make it true.

1 Mount Elbrus is the second-highest peak in Europe.

2 West Caucasian turs are unique to the Mount Elbrus region.

3 Dragonwort roots can be used for medicinal purposes.

4 No children have summited Mount Elbrus.

5 An important Balkar skill is knowing how to make jewelry.

6 There have been avalanches on Mount Elbrus, but no mudslides.

ANSWERS

1. False. Mount Elbrus is the highest peak in Europe. **2.** True. They live in the rugged mountain, cliff, and meadow areas just below the snow line of Mount Elbrus. **3.** True. They can be used to stop bleeding, as an antibacterial, and to treat digestive issues. **4.** False. Jordan Romero was the first boy to summit, at age 10, and Jaahnavi Sriperambuduru was the first girl to summit, at age 13. **5.** False. One of the most important skills that Balkars learn is knitting. **6.** False. There was a mudslide in the area in 2017.

Short Answer

Answer the following questions using information from the book.

1. How many glaciers does Mount Elbrus have?
2. Which Mount Elbrus summit is higher?
3. Who was the first person to reach Mount Elbrus's eastern summit?
4. How many different species of plants are in the Mount Elbrus region?
5. What are two main threats to the Mount Elbrus area?

Multiple Choice

Choose the best answer for the following questions.

1. How high is Mount Elbrus's western summit?
   a. 18,510 feet (5,642 m)
   b. 12,500 feet (3,810 m)
   c. 6,562 feet (2,000 m)

2. Who wrote *The Frosty Caucasus* about his Mount Elbrus expedition?
   a. Jordan Romero
   b. Florence Crauford Grove
   c. Horace Walker

3. Which flowering plant grows in the Mount Elbrus region?
   a. Bluebell
   b. Marigold
   c. Rhododendron

4. Which extreme sport takes place on Mount Elbrus?
   a. Sand kiting
   b. Skyrunning
   c. Bungee jumping

Activity

Make a Glacier

Glaciers like the ones on Mount Elbrus form when new snow builds onto old snow and transforms into ice. Each new layer of snow buries and compresses the older layers. Try making a glacier to see how it looks as it forms and moves rocks when it melts.

Materials

Freezer

Two clear plastic cups

Water

Sand and gravel

Shallow dish

Instructions

1. Pour 1 inch (2 cm) of water into one of the clear plastic cups. Put it in the freezer and let it sit overnight.

2. Remove the cup from the freezer and pour 0.5 inches (1 cm) of water on top of the ice. Add some sand and gravel, then return it to the freezer.

3. Once the mixture has frozen, add another 0.5 inches (1 cm) of water, as well as some sand and gravel to your cup. Refreeze.

4. Press 1 inch (2 cm) of sand into the other plastic cup. Run the frozen cup under warm water until the "glacier" pops out. Put it on top of the sand in the second cup and freeze. Recycle the first plastic cup.

5. Run the frozen cup under warm water to release the glacier. Examine the layers. Is there a difference between the older ice and the newer ice?

6. Let the glacier melt in the shallow dish. What happens to the rocks as the ice melts?

Key Words

altitudes: the measurements above sea level of different locations on Earth

crevasses: deep open cracks, especially in a glacier

crust: top layer of Earth where landmasses and oceans are located

dictator: a ruler with total power over a country, who has not been elected

dormant: temporarily inactive

ecosystem: all living and non-living things in an area

elevation: height above sea level

glaciers: enormous, slow-moving chunks of ice

herbivores: animals that eat only plants

lava: hot, liquid rock that flows from a volcano

lichens: tiny, plant-like organisms that can grow in harsh conditions

Nazi: a member of a political party controlling Germany from 1933 to 1945

nocturnal: active at night

saddle: a pass or ridge that slopes between two mountain peaks

species: a group of closely related living organisms

Titan: any of the children of Uranus and Gaea, and their descendants

vertebrate: referring to an animal that has a backbone or spinal column

Index

Log on to www.av2books.com

AV² by Weigl brings you media enhanced books that support active learning. Go to www.av2books.com, and enter the special code found on page 2 of this book. You will gain access to enriched and enhanced content that supplements and complements this book. Content includes video, audio, weblinks, quizzes, a slideshow, and activities.

AV² Online Navigation

Audio
Listen to sections of the book read aloud.

Book Pages
AV² pages directly correspond to pages in the book.

Video
Watch informative video clips.

Key Words
Study vocabulary, and complete a matching word activity.

Embedded Weblinks
Gain additional information for research.

Try This!
Complete activities and hands-on experiments.

Quizzes
Test your knowledge.

Slideshow
View images and captions, and prepare a presentation.

AV² was built to bridge the gap between print and digital. We encourage you to tell us what you like and what you want to see in the future.

Sign up to be an AV² Ambassador at www.av2books.com/ambassador.